A Sparkles Production

"The Story of my Life"

Courtney N. Lazalier

(A.K.A) Sparkles

INSPIRED BY

DAN THE MAN, MOMMOM (A.K.A) PATRICIA BLACK/GADDIS, MY PARENTS SCOTT
AND RUSHELL LAZALIER, AND TO EVERYONE ELSE WHO HAS TAKEN THE TIME IN
HELPING RAISE ME; GRANDMA JOANIE (A.K.A) EVA JOAN PATTILLO/JOHNSON,
TRACEY HARGET, PEE-WEE WHITE & MORGAN, ALETHEA WHITE, MISSY ROSS, AND
MISSY AND STEVE ROACH.

ALSO A SPECIAL THANKS TO MY FRIENDS AND THE REST OF MY FAMILY AS WELL AS
GRANNY KAREN AND PAP (A.K.A) JEAN HILL, TO ONE OF MY
COUNSELORS MISTY DODSON, ALSO OF COURSE MY SON CARSON MATTHEW
TINSLEY AND AS WELL TO THE REST OF HIS FAMILY.

WITHOUT ALL OF THESE PEOPLE I WOULDN'T HAVE BEEN ABLE TO CREATE, "A
SPARKLES PRODUCTION, - THE STORY OF MY LIFE."

CONTENTS

.

ACKNOWLEDGMENTS

I would like to acknowledge allpoetry.com for allowing me the opportunity in writing poetry to enter into their contests. Giving me inspiration and the ideal topics on some of the poems I've written. Also I would like to acknowledge createspace.com for allowing me to becomes a publisher and author creating and selling my book of poetry. I'm deeply appreciative and give gratitude towards both websites.

1 HER VOICES

No one hears as she screams inside,

With feelings she tries so hard to hide.

Once again her world has fallen apart,

Only to conclude a broken heart.

With tears she smiles no more,

Because she let him through the door.

Her hearts valves have too much pressure,

Now they only share displeasure.

These emotions she tries so hard to conceal,

Are all on display to show how she must feel.

With shattered hopes and dreams,

Fate appears to be not only how it seems.

They're intravenously intertwined and with blood shot eyes

She wishes to scream without anyone hearing her cries.

Her feelings she can't hide much longer,

She wants to prove that she is stronger.

Revealing under her well kept hidden mask,

True colors leak out ruining that very task.

Thoughts keep racing in her head,

Replaying everything he ever said.

Trying to drown out these voices,

She's now up to face new choices.

Insanity is left open for debate,

Emotions went from love and happy to anger and hate.

If she screams out to loud,

In victory her voices will be proud.

She's already fallen to deep,

Her smile is now harder to keep.

As the tarot cards play out as they were dealt,

There revealing her future and pain she has felt.

The dice keep spinning,

But it seems like the voices may be winning.

Love; hate, joy; pain, yin and yang,

There's empty spaces where the frames use to hang

Trying to keep him out of sight and out of mind,

Searching for answers she may never find.

Wondering if he was ever truly a friend,

Or actually a stranger playing pretend.

So much time together and so many memories made,

That will last forever and never fade.

She forgives way to quickly and forgets grudges.

A true sweetheart, but she is carless and he always judges.

Both are at fault and to blame,

Equally tired of playing this twisted mind game.

Its left open for debate to compromise and be put to the test,

Because in each other they bring out the worst and the best.

Or surrender and both take different paths.

Never forgetting a moment they shared or there laughs,

Turning their lessons learned into wisdom to share.

Forever friends never forgetting they do care.

Once each other's second half,

In a relationship but now taking a different path.

They will love each other forever,

Because they share a lifetime of memories together.

(the rest is up to them to decide

Living life to its fullest to enjoy the ride)

2 CAPTURED BY THE MOON LIGHTS SPELL (A 40 WORD PICTURE PROMPT)

In the silent, cool, midnight air

No one in sight except for the pair

Careless, young, and looking for lust

Hopeful to unmask an unfamiliar sense of trust

Sorrows disappearing till' sunrise,

Enlightening both with inner-peace till' the moon dies.

3 AN ETERNAL GOODBYE FORCED BY THE GODS OF THE SEA

Somewhere in the mist of glacial chaos,

The waves of the ocean become the new boss.

Moving violently and forcing intense arctic blows to the head,

Piercing into their body and souls making all life seem dead.

All he wanted was to hear a sweet faint tonality of chimes,

But instead he was left with traces of her voice to seem more like a mimes.

Scared because his 20/20 vision was now like glass in need of rain-ex.

His life was perfect till storm hit way and now it seemed more complex.

devoted and eager in finding his partner of a life time,

who vanished like the flash of a dime.

Before his worst fear became reality of her being sent above.

Too much pressure on his hearts valves were now making his emotion evolve,

Making his tears fall like rain and now realizing the puzzle he must solve.

Glimpse of something as white as snow caught his eye,

Bringing a non-familiar drop in the pit of his stomach making him sigh.

Louder than thunder there was a yell that echoed through the night air,

And he couldn't bring himself to move all he could do was stare.

Finally courage and his sense of survival made his actions change,

Fighting against the waves he swam to the object that seemed so strange.

It was suddenly true that reality had became his worst fear,

Her eyes that use to be full of color and life now seemed cold and clear.

Looking away and then back again it became apparent she never looked away,

Never blinking and just like a statue she was motionless leaving him with nothing to say.

Knowing that even if he did have his true love wouldn't reply

And without question he knew exactly the reason why.

As desperate as he wanted life's cruel ways to not be real,

It was evident the grim reaper had his true love on his list of life's to steal.

It was now time for this man to say his last words in order for her to rest in peace.

As an everlasting eternal goodbye and with sorrow in his voice he whispered,

" I Love You, Reese."

4 WHAT COMES NEXT

The curious mind questions what is after life as we know it?

Does today's actions determine going to heaven or the devils pit?

Basically the old saying, "what comes around, goes around" is true.

Every act is taken into consideration in order to know what to do.

I also believe that reincarnation plays a part of what happens next,

Even though it isn't proven or written in the bibles text.

Maybe karma really isn't just intended for this life we live in,

Multiple life's would make an easier decision when asking, did we sin?

Was there one unforgivable sin that ruined all chances of going above?

A decision made by a fallen child who could change his mind with love?

How can only one lifetime determine everything?

Some people are left with such short life to be denied an angels wing,

If this is true then why are some people's only answer suicide?

Is life so terrible your left the unforgivable sin instead of enjoying the ride?

If reincarnation is real how do you know that the next life will be better?

It could be worse than the reason you wrote the suicide letter,

Whenever god comes like a thief in the night

He's going to be considerably judgmental deciding if your sin was alright.

Determining the golden gates or burning pit based by every action you made.

Every moment he will consider making it not just some memory meant to fade.

Do good and in the end good will come to you.

It will help Karma's actions and eternally too.

5 REWRITING HER ENDING TO FIT

Misunderstood and misguided still their love story is her favorite.

Falling faster and Swifter than Smokey and the Bandit,

Role Playing and scheming Smoother than Bonnie and Clyde,

And Thought to be Stronger than the need of entitling her as his bride

Blindsided and young she still has a lot to learn,

He's already won a broken heart but now it's her turn.

while he insists on knowing the ending and collecting the pieces of his past,

she knows the ending has yet been written, implying he reads too fast.

Young and dumb but smarter than Juliet,

Her intentions are to make an impression he win never forget.

She has good Looks and is pretty with a permanent smile,

Still he acts like an ogre insisting that is not his Style.

Lost and Alienated he's in need to find home,

realizing he's no longer in Kansas anymore appearing to look like A Nome.

With Armor And Shield he's fooled this princess As being Prince charming,

Now after kissing this Bullfrog new impressions have started alarming.

Not awakened by his enchanted kiss but actually by his immoral spell,
She now feels like a lost mermaid who's only life-line is a seashell.
He's motivated like the Wolf racing Lil' Red Riding Hood to her house,
Now seeming like a Tall Tale and leaving her lost like Fievel the Mouse.

Looking in the mirror asking himself, "who's the fairest of them all?"
Reflected back seven dwarf girls making one shine like a crystal ball.
Realizing who but unable to remember by name who had real humble soft skin,
Hoped to beat midnight's spell from turning his sweet pumpkin back again.

He had determination and intentions like the Lil' Engine That Could,
This time he was kneeling sizing her shoe to fit already knowing it would.
Her being Sweet like Thumbelina couldn't help from being small and kind,
By implying his buried treasure was no longer in need to search and find.

Realizing that What he thought to be like the Pink Panther to her heart
Was wrong making their ending not like he intended from the start.
But like Peter Pan and the Lost Boys in need of finding their home.
All thanks to that girl who took the time to write and read him this poem.

6 FAME WON'T BUY HIS HEART
(9 line max picture prompt)

Depressed and disheartened she's confused by her sorrow

Money, fame, and power is evident to still exist tomorrow

She has everything anyone could want except for now his isn't here

Perhaps fame and fortune won't always make her tears disappear

Beauty and the family name obviously won't be able to fix this

Her spoiled and greedy qualities definitely weren't a favorite of his

So now he's vanished, and he won't tolerate her selfish way of life

Consequently implying he no longer wants this princess as his wife

7 AN ANGELS ENCOUNTER

Angels are cleverly disguised

Admirably innocent and rarely despised

Appearing at first as only a stranger

Actually to fool your sense of danger

Another sparkle to brighten your days

Advising to change all your evil ways

Adorable and never selfish

Accomplishing every desire and wish

Actually projecting for real just like in your dreams

Accountable like stitches in a quilt's seams

Astonishing and respectful but never arrogant

Assumed to be your special angel that was heaven sent

8 BROKEN PROMISES OR FALSE INTENSIONS?

Life is intentionally unknown

Beautiful disasters in mine seem to be prone

Broken promises are failed intensions

Made by false insinuations

leaving my expectations low

a predetermined answer that I already know

making all emotions invisible for anyone to see

an arousal no one will witness out of me

giving everyone the benefit of the doubt

no matter the outcome you'll never hear me shout

focused by this routine of common let down

drives my devotion of changing the common frown

making the difference is my first step to this goal

heartwarming motives that touch your soul

faithful, loyal, trustworthy, and probably his only friend

opposing from most I offer my hand to lend

pushing everything i already know aside

I allowed you to prove that you care and really actually tried

was never judgmental nor could i put my guard down

ignoring the usual gossip that comes along with our town

giving you trust knowing that it wasn't easy to come by

still I patiently waited only to be proven that is was all a lie

Broken intentions that I was your only one

Never really knowing until 2 years was said and done

Complete opposites was something I found us to be

Upset of course but never a complete surprise to me

Just like any other person I've met

Something I could have probably won if I placed my bet

Unfortunately I promised I wouldn't judge you

Giving you all the room to show me something new

Your devotion of showing me the difference

Now after patiently waiting doesn't really make sense

You promised to be faithful and true

Blindsided I took on that notion too

Broken intensions you couldn't help but share

But that wasn't my idea of showing that I care

After a lifetime of memories and a baby on the way

Now you tell me things leaving me speechless on what to say

Seems like the life you have chosen after becoming a free man

Like usual stopped life in its track just when it began

Insisting your rather taste in a common whore

That you couldn't help but adore

Instead of the common house wife

Proved to be the leading cause of the prison life

Sometimes instead of teaching what you thought you knew

Listening to others should have been on your list to do

I preached that there was a reason people weren't in your spot

Slowing your role without the fame would have meant a lot

Becoming the difference you promised to be

Was just another broken intension for me to see

Not impressed by your false charm you showed so well

Confused by it I'll admit in love I fell

Another lesson learned but not a regret

Just another stranger I met

But just the same don't be confused by me

When an arousal isn't something you'll get to see

Because I wear a mask that is pretty clever too

Just in a different way that you do

Still confident and eager to go forward

Don't be mistaken because your someone I always adored

Memories will always be imprinted on my mind

but these common qualities in people i seem to always find

hopefully this wasn't just some lesson you were trying to teach

because I've already learned this lesson you tried to preach

common failure isn't going to change me

I'll still be open minded towards who the next guy might be

always giving the benefit of the doubt without putting my guard down

and this will just be another gossip story in our small little town

I love you and ill always miss you more than you know

Love always your sweetheart a memory time ago

.

9 NOT A DELUSION, BUT AN ILLUSION.

Things aren't always as they seem

don't confuse reality with a dream

maybe the situation is really just another illusion

set out to seem like just another delusion

reflecting something different or to seem insane

that is actually just simple and plane

knowing the backing and warrants behind your reasons

that are hard to find as they're lost behind all the seasons

as time passed so swiftly before realizing they were lost

affording more than what you thought they would cost

perhaps your living life in a dream of astral projection

ignoring your actual life and losing everything that needed protection

living life in a faded transparent daze without anything real

leaving your life to be just another dream that time couldn't help but steal

as it snuck around like a thief in the night

it was gone before you could blink like it was never in sight

hopefully you'll hurry open your eyes before it's too late

everything you could have had so easily might become something they hate

don't let it pass you or confuse something you already know

define who you are by not letting the illusion tell you so

but by showing who you are and what you preach to be

your true beliefs and ideas are far better than the dreams you see

I know this to be true by listening to your dreams and to you preach

proving your dreams are illusions and there's a much better person you teach

10 AN EVERLASTING FLAME

Do you remember the first night we met?

Or how I use to take pictures of the sun set?

Remember laying in my bed?

Seductive thoughts uncontrollably racing through your head?

Having someone listen to your stories?

Or the nights we cuddled without any cares or worries?

Remember how good it felt in complete silence?

Both pulses racing making each other's heart beats more intense?

Drowning out all problems leaving only our whispers left to embrace?

Both feeling wanted and never out of place?

Synched into one another making us feel complete?

Some kind of warm fire that burned its own kind of heat?

A kind that is hard to find,

Not an evil flame but one that gave a peace of mind?

Enchanted with a sense of knowing,

A spark that couldn't help from growing.

Into a blitz feeding fire starting from just a flame,

That only us two could tame?

Being that we were each other's neutrals and negatives,

Eliminating everything bad to make it all positives?

A Complete, inseparable, unbreakable, relationship,

That was a permanent friendship?

Eternally burned in each other's hearts and minds,

A kind that most people search a lifetime and never finds?

Of course you do because it still has burning coals

That even I can't deny as it's still a small flame between our souls

That will never be simply blown out with just one breath

Its eternal until both life's are taken by death

Maybe even further more into another life time

Created into another enzyme

making it an ever-lasting flame,

that we were the only ones to blame.

ABOUT THE AUTHOR

All my life I have been through many good and bad experiences. All equally combined as being beautiful privileges, resulting to my simply perfectly imperfect self. because of these privileges they've all came together making me who I am today. Its easily shown as these character traits I have bleed though showing the world my sense of existence. Too many flaws show that I am clumsy, I'm accident prone, I lack common sense, trust no one, and deny my true feelings. Which of course I don't have any thoughts as being a bad thing to have flaws. because everyone has them, no one is flawless. I also will admit i love to truly, which I'm not ashamed of. I give my heart to freely to others to fast. Easily I find myself caring too much for others. As a down fall I leave myself open to get hurt to easily. A lot of what has made me who i am today are those who i have love for. Although they have made it a custom to continue to put my high hopes of them to shame, I'll admit I forgive too quickly. Also ill say they've at the same time left me with memories that later on i find myself laughing to oftcn at. guud or bad I easily find myself to always forgive and forget grudges. maybe reason being that I give everyone the benefit of the doubt and have too much consideration towards every one. of course everyone makes mistakes especially I. Rather someone has left a good or bad mark in my life, I never expect or assume that the next person is going to be that way or the next outcome. basically I live life open mindedly. Always considering the worst and the best. therefore I am not to be let down, or have too much hope. At the same time though I'll always be surprised whenever something good comes my way. leaving a smile on my face. rough child hood some could say play a huge factor in who I am today. moving often I transfer every other semester. one reason being my mom's been to prison five times. As a early mother I gave birth to my beautiful son Carson at age 18. I partied more than I should and was raised in a bar. at the same time I also had good influences as well; a good loving mother and father who tried giving me nothing but the best. Also I was granted to having many different points of views by surrounding myself by many different types of families.

respecting others was a must in order to continue my welcome. enjoying the small

things and friends were easy to come by, making me a people person. Everybody has a

different story, it's up to each person to make sure they don't let anyone else hold the

pen while writing it. my friends and family have influenced me making my life a

beautiful privileges. I am who I am today and have strong beliefs creating me into

becoming this strange unique libertarian that I am today. the rest is still unwritten

only for someone to later on read, while smiling remembering everything she ever

said. mainly because if the presence of my being has forced a smile upon your face

then my goal in life has been achieved. Resulting as an accomplishment, showing

that i have successfully came at peace. peace at mind that is. I'm just a child trying to

figure it all out one day and one obstacle at a time.

-Peace,

Courtney N. Lazalier (A.K.A) Sparkles